© 2017 by Barbour Publishing, Inc.

Print ISBN 978-1-68322-339-9

All rights reserved. No part of this publication may be reproduced or transmitted for commercial purposes, except for brief quotations in printed reviews, without written permission of the publisher.

Cover illustration: Emma Segal
Interior illustrations: Yee Von Chan, Emma Segal, and Chelen Ecija

All scripture quotations are taken from the King James Version of the Bible.

Published by Barbour Books, an imprint of Barbour Publishing, Inc., P.O. Box 719, Uhrichsville, OH 44683, www.barbourbooks.com

Our mission is to inspire the world with the life-changing message of the Bible.

Printed in the United States of America.

BARBOUR BOOKS
An Imprint of Barbour Publishing, Inc.

Thy Word is a lamp unto my feet, and a light unto my path.

Psalm 119:105

Delight thyself also in the Lord:
and he shall give thee the desires of thine heart.

Psalm 37:4

The Lord

is my light and my salvation;
whom shall I fear?
the Lord is the strength of my life;
of whom shall I be afraid?

Psalm 27:1

THE WORDS OF THE LORD

PSALM 12:6

ARE PURE WORDS

O TASTE AND SEE THAT THE LORD IS GOOD.

PSALM 34:8

My help cometh from the Lord which made heaven and earth.

PSALM 121:2

CAST THY BURDEN UPON THE LORD, and HE SHALL SUSTAIN THEE.

psalm 55:22

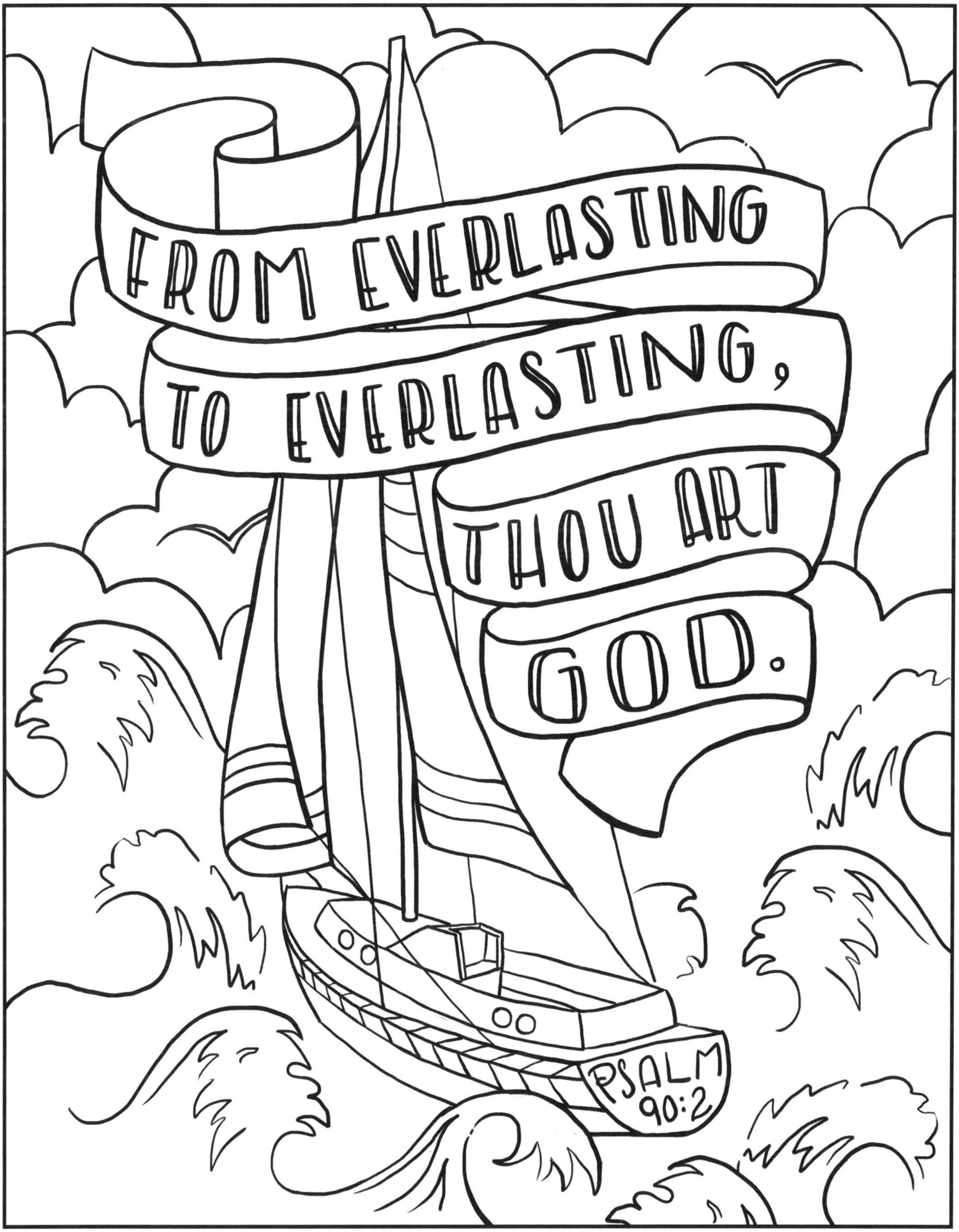
FROM EVERLASTING
TO EVERLASTING,
THOU ART
GOD.
PSALM 90:2

O come, let us worship and bow down: let us kneel before the LORD our maker.

PSALM 95:6

By the Word of the Lord were the Heavens made.

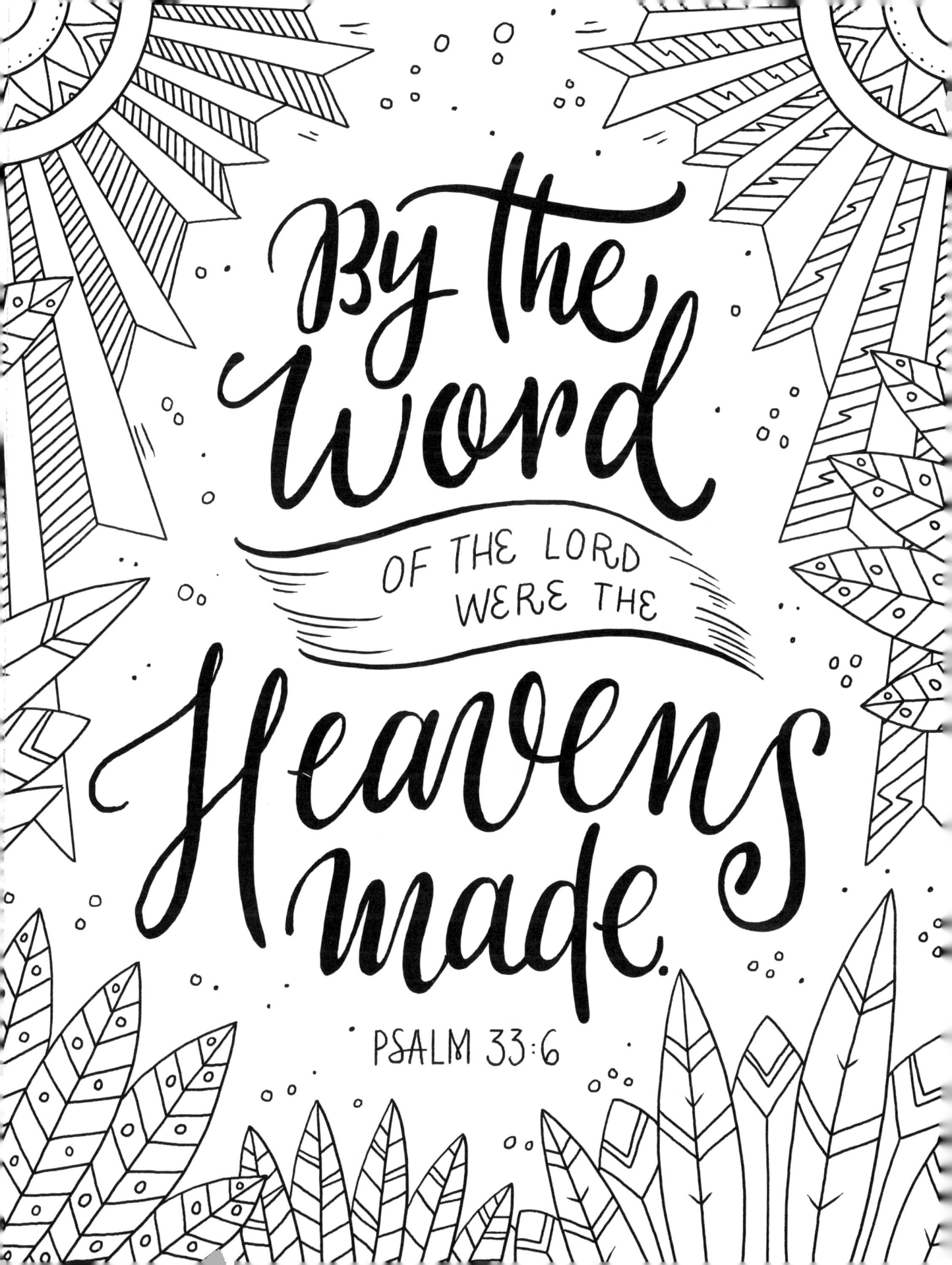

PSALM 33:6

But the SALVATION of the righteous is of the Lord: he is their STRENGTH in the time of TROUBLE.

Psalm 37:39

The LORD is KING for ever and ever.

PSALM 10:16

Bless the Lord, O my Soul.

Psalm 103:22

It is **GOD** that... *maketh my* WAY *perfect.*

Psalm 18:32

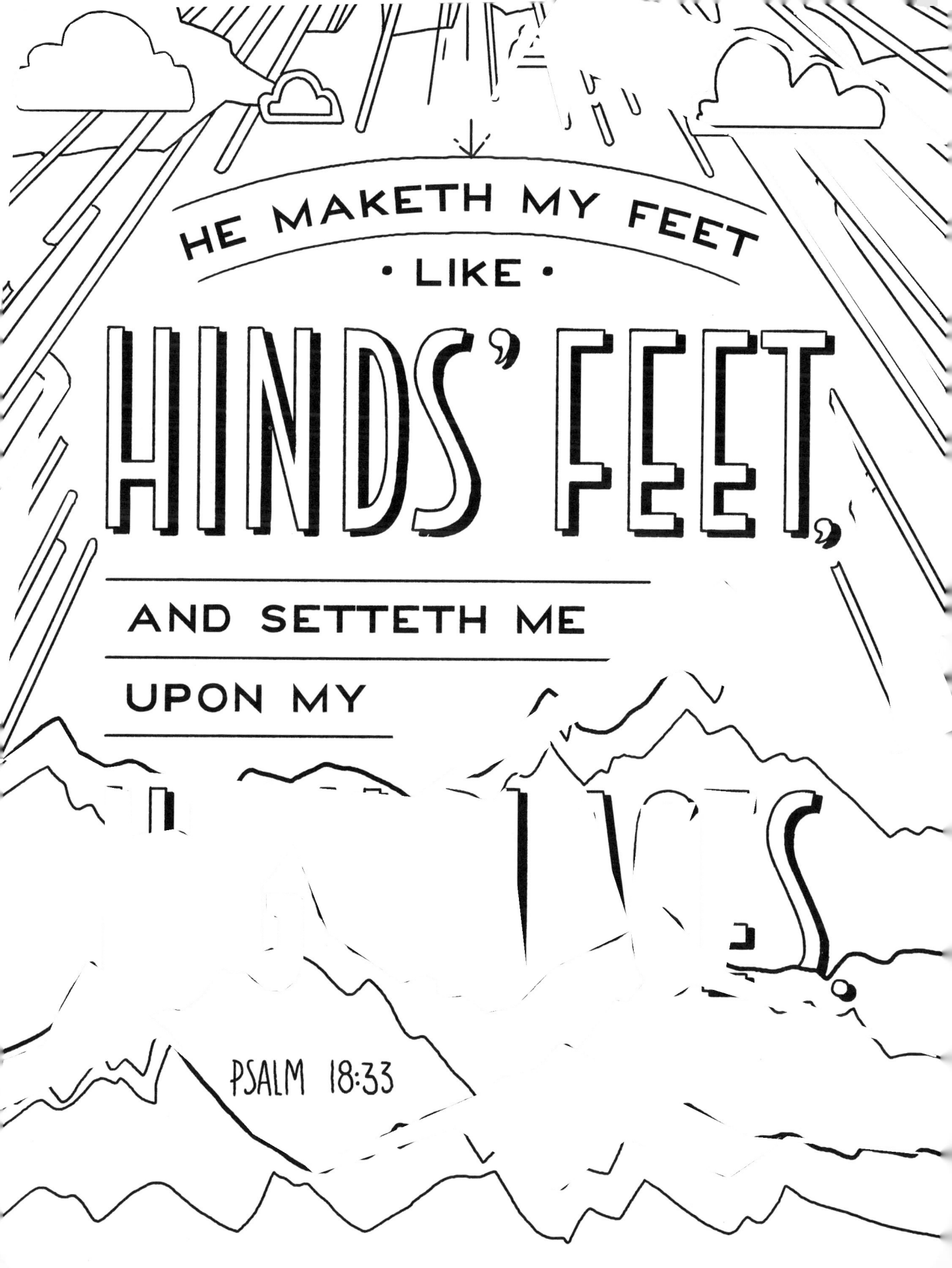

HE MAKETH MY FEET
· LIKE ·
HINDS' FEET,
AND SETTETH ME
UPON MY

PSALM 18:33

Return, O Lord, deliver my soul.

Psalm 6:4

O GIVE **THANKS** unto the Lord; for he is **GOOD;** because his **MERCY** ENDURETH FOR EVER.

Psalm 118:1